To

Pastor George Robinson

Thank God for y
on March the third Sunday
that you God has fit me in the
world install me in the
Year 1988. Take care and
may your work speak for your Preach
will live up to what your
Be don season.
out of season.

Love Pastor Kim
I Robinson Kim
10-11-2017
Lakeland
hospital
mother
his

I Believed Him

It was easy for me to believe God,
because I could believe my father!

JAMES L. HINES

WESTBOW
PRESS®
A DIVISION OF THOMAS NELSON
& ZONDERVAN

Scripture taken from the King James Version of the Bible.

WestBow Press books may be ordered through booksellers or by contacting:

WestBow Press
A Division of Thomas Nelson & Zondervan
1663 Liberty Drive
Bloomington, IN 47403
www.westbowpress.com
1 (866) 928-1240

ISBN: 978-1-5127-9466-3 (sc)
ISBN: 978-1-5127-9467-0 (hc)
ISBN: 978-1-5127-9494-6 (e)

Library of Congress Control Number: 2017910932

Print information available on the last page.

WestBow Press rev. date: 07/28/2017

Acknowledgment

First, I would like to thank God for giving me the personal and pastoral experiences I have had over the years, and for allowing me to mature and help other to mature also. I thank my wife, Leontyne, for her love, support and patience. I thank my son and daughter for their faithfulness to the ministry and the Hines name, which has allowed me to better serve in the role of pastor. I thank my church family for helping me with rearing my children, especially Charles and Irene Estelle, James and Chlorita Conner, Charles and Olympthy Arnold, Albert and Minnie Peterson, Willie and Eric Baldwin, Russell and Brenda Davis, Theresa Travis, Maurice and Jolita Burton, Donald and Mary Sanders, Nathan and Barbara Gibbs, Larry and Valerie Bullen, Anthony Hurst, Cldye and Pat Robinson and Tom and Linda Brown.

I want to especially thank God for those who helped me in the ministry: Pastor Nathan Crout, Pastor Namon and Viola Kline, Pastor Jerome Kirby, Pastor Lightfoot, Pastor Otha Gilliard, Pastor

A.P. Williams, Pastor C.M. Jones, Bishop Fred Cunningham, Bishop Roger Jones, Pastor James Cooper. Pastor Arcellius Flanagan, Rosetta Harrell, Ruth Walker, Jackie Barbier, Mattie Quinn, John and Mary Parker, Rose White, Willie and Laura Morgan, Emma Huston, Joseph Dunigan and Family, Clarine Person, Robert Hill J.C. Allen, Roy Buckner, Susan Holmes, Heather Stilfer and Pastor George and Goergia Wade.

I want to thank Pastor Bennie and Brenda Gibson, Minster Ronnie Hall, Pastor Coye and Keturah Boyer, Minster Michael and Felonia Scott, and Minister Melvin and Joyce Hicks for being great associate ministers. I would also like to thank the parents who allowed their children to spend nights at our home. They were the seed planted to give birth to the Lily Missions Center. Thank God for James and Cherry Nash, Colonel Richard Nash, Bob Russell, Jim & Jonas McCluskey, and Louis Glick Family.

I thank God for the two father's, Pastor Joe Hines and Sammy Smith, and the two mothers, Flora Hines and Allene Smith, He gave me.

Finally, I would like to thank all of the Jackson Community for supporting me with my life's work.

Foreword
By Dr. Doug Wilcoxson

When I moved to Michigan in 2014 to work at Spring Arbor University, I had a variety of people mention I should get to know Reverend Jimmy Hines. These people were community leaders, business leaders, politicians, educators, medical professionals, clergy and more. They all had interactions with this man and his ministries, and were influenced by the work that was being done by him personally or through his church. My first meeting with Rev. Hines was at a foundation board meeting which was characterized by wanting to inspire, innovate and involve the community to make it a better place. Rev. Hines sat quietly for the first hour of the meeting.

My entire working life has been in Christian Higher Education. One of my roles for over 20 years was supervising the chaplain of the university – the person responsible for shaping the spiritual life and the chapel program for the university community. I have heard the most powerful people and best speakers in the world during my professional career, including over 1,500 inspirational speakers and pastors. People like President George H. Bush, Prime Minister Tony Blair, Condoleezza Rice, Tony Dungy, Josh McDowell, Margaret Thatcher, Franklin Graham and so many more. I almost always wondered after hearing them speak, who they really are in moments of crisis and quiet. I wondered what they really believed that informed their behavior.

I characterize Rev Hines this way. The more I get to know him the more I want to get to know him. You see, I have learned the more in depth I have gotten to know my dear friend and brother, that there is a strong consistency of life and obedience to what he believes. He lives out, in profound ways, what he believes is true. It's not that others do not, it is just that he is bold and radical in doing what is right. This makes me increasingly curious to know him more.

This book gives a glimpse into the ways that Rev Hines has been powerfully used by God. Rev. Hines is not without fault, but he consistently seeks to listen to how the Holy Spirit is guiding him and then he acts! This book will inspire you and encourage you to know Rev. Hines more. But even more important it will imbed a deep curiosity to know the God he serves. It will encourage and challenge you to act on what you know is right.

In that first foundation meeting where I first met Rev Hines, when he did speak, it was with a depth of insight about the organizations that serve the greater Jackson Community. It was with wisdom about where dollars could best help the community. It was with conviction and compassion for serving individuals and changing systems that need help. It was with a belief that God will use even one person who is faithful. HE BELIEVES!

Preface

In writing this book, my prayer is that it will glorified God and help those who are struggling with hearing God's voice. I was given great advice by one of my preacher friends, Pastor Terrance King. He said, "The greatest point of our witness is the place where God has delivered us." I am writing out of a sense that God has called me to do this writing. Writing is not my strength, but obedience is. I pray that my struggles and successes will encourage others to study God's word, realizing that the blessing is in the struggle, according to Psalms 119:71. I would like to share the words of a few who saw the book developing. Glorise Peterson, office manager, said "you wrote the book and proved the book". Jimmie McCan Sr., a widower, commented, "You have given so much to this city now you are giving to this country." I pray that people would understand that God perfects people in the dark room to develop the picture they will present to the world.

Please be encouraged to obey God and not your heart, Jeremiah 17:9. If God has called you to build, then build. But, please do not build based on a desire to be like others. I shared struggles with success hoping that those who are going through difficult times will keep the faith to overcome them.

Introduction
I Believed

This is a story about a young man who has faith in his father who could not read or write, but pastored a church. He sought his father's advice about marriage, which turned out to be good advice and yielded the result he was seeking. The young man later hears God direct him to pastor a church, which eventually led to building a new structure through exercising his faith in God. His faith in his earthly father made it easy for him to believe he was hearing God's voice. This book is called I Believed *Him,* because I believed God and brought every thought into captivity to the obedience of Christ in four distinct areas of my life: marriage, church, finance, and family. Within each section, I'm going to leave a biblical blueprint using Scripture to show how God inspired me; ordering my steps in His Word to help me create a document that wll enable me to be a blessing to the Kingdom. My desire is to exalt the Savior, equip the saint, and evangelize the sinner.

Many pastors have encouraged me to write this book. Ironically, many encouraged me by saying, "Please don't take this information to the grave." Pastor Lance Chaney from Florida—a friend, in particular—is included in this group. He is the late pastor of the St. John's Baptist Church in West Palm, Florida. Pastor Chaney has gone home to be with the Lord. My hope is to honor his memory in this book. I'm thankful to God for Pastor Chaney's belief in me.

All Scripture references are from the King James Version of the Bible. I want the audience to be able to read it and find the information rapidly. As Jesus told Judas, "Go do what you must quickly." There are some things we must get done now.

At the beginning of this book, it's imperative to indicate how God works in a complete circle. I arrived at Lily Missionary Baptist church, where I am now the pastor, because of a very gifted woman, who worked with me at a local energy company. She typed my résumé and sent it to Lily Baptist Church when the position of pastor was vacant.

Twenty-five years later, I met a very gifted lady named Cindy and her husband at a local restaurant. Cindy convinced me to start writing this book and graciously volunteered to transcribe this manuscript. Ironically, Cindy and Helen worked for the same energy company that

I worked for during the same time period. We completed the rough draft and emailed it off, waiting on its return.

While waiting, Cindy passed away from a heart attack. I pray this document will bless others and assist them in the performance of their Kingdom work. God bless all of you.

CHAPTER 1

Marriage

The Mystery of Marriage

Marriage started with Adam and Eve. In the beginning Adam was alone, and he needed a wife. Adam had to sacrifice a rib to receive a wife. The wife had to reverence her husband. In other words, remember what Ephesians 5:33 says: "Let every husband love his wife and let every wife reverence her husband." I contend that if Eve had just told Satan, "You need to talk to my husband," she would have reverenced her husband, and Adam could have taken care of Satan. But thank God for His grace.

I learned this truth in my own marriage. I fell in love when I first saw Leontyne Smith when I was in the eighth grade and she was in the seventh. She was my middle-school sweetheart. She was so beautiful to me, but she didn't have the crush on me that I had on her. But as my father would always say, "Pray like it depends on God and work like it depends on you." One Sunday I asked him how to get a wife. He told me, "You pray for a wife." So I began to pray. My whole eighth grade year went by, and she never once smiled at me. I remembered the words of my father: "Pray like it depends on God and work like it depends on you."

My mother drove a bus for the local public school system. Leontyne and I were both riders. My mother kept her bus at home, so I made a bargain with her. I agree to clean her bus if she would take a new route picking up all other riders first and picking up Leontyne last. This plan worked. When we picked up Leontyne, the bus was crowded with only one seat that was open. That seat happened to be right by me, and for the next four years, she was always forced to sit beside me. I was so much in love with her that I would walk back and forth in front of her house, as she lived down the street. Her sister would look outside and say to Leontyne, "Would you at least look outside so this boy could go home?"

Leontyne and I started dating when she was in the tenth grade and I was in the eleventh. I was on the Benton Harbor High School basketball team. I will never forget February 24, 1979. I asked her to be my girlfriend, and she said she would think about it. But, as I walked away, she said, "Yes." We dated through high school and into college. She attended Michigan State University and I attended Central Michigan University. While in college, I walked and hitchhiked 66 miles to visit her one evening.

What a life I've had. Leontyne supported me in many ways. She is my best friend and brought strong family values to our marriage. Her mother a twin, is a very beautiful woman. Her father is a very upstanding African-American man in our community. He was the housing commissioner and also owned a bar, called the Zodiac Club. He and I were always engaged in religious conversations—no debates, just sharing. One day he asked me what my intentions were for his daughter. When I was in the eleventh grade, I responded to him that I wanted to marry her.

He put me in the car, drove me out into the country, and pulled up to a little house. He walked me up to the house. This old woman came outside, and he said to me, "Can you love this old woman?"

I looked at this woman and said, "What?"

He said, "This is what Leontyne is going to look like when she is 70."

I kept my word that I would stay with Leontyne until she looked like her grandmother. Mr. Smith was a very strong figure in my life.

Call to Preach

While attending Central Michigan University, I tried to kill myself, because I didn't want to preach. This was my junior year, the season for direction. I struggled with God's assignment for my life. Oh, how Satan keeps us from seeing tomorrow. It was April 11 at 11:05 p.m. when I pulled a gun out of my desk drawer. My roommate opened the bedroom door. He didn't see the gun, but he spoke these words: "Try God." It was a life-changing statement.

I later went to class and confessed in the classroom that God had called me to preach. After I left the class, heading back to the dorm, it began to rain. I asked God, "What is happening?" It was only raining around me. He spoke to me and said, "The angels of heaven are happy." I went to my room, called my father. When I told my father what had happened, he scheduled my first sermon.

CHAPTER 2

Church

The Mystery of Marriage and the Church (Ephesians 5:32)

At the age of twenty-five, in October 1987, I was installed as the interim pastor of the Lily Missionary Baptist Church. I replaced the famous Reverend Dr. George Wade, who had died of a massive heart attack six months earlier, in March 1987. My life in Jackson, Michigan, had started on June 30, 1986. I was hired at a local utility company as a program analyst. The only transportation I had was the family car, which broke down on I-94 as I was headed to my hometown. I eventually caught a ride as I was hitchhiking down the road. A young white male with a big Labrador Retriever picked me up and drove approximately 75 miles to my parents' front steps. When I returned to work the following Monday, I had no transportation, so I walked to work which was about five miles.

While at work, a young man approached me. At the time I didn't know his name, and he asked me, "Are you a preacher?" I told him yes, but I didn't want anyone to know that. I wanted to go to work and go home. He looked at me and said God had told him to give me his car. I received his car, and every Friday he would gas it up for me.

Well, one month in 1987—I believe it was about January—I purchased a car and returned his car. My car cost $900. It was a green 1971 station wagon. Out of kindness, the same young man invited me to go to a church with him, and I responded by saying yes. As I was sitting in the back of the church, the late Reverend George Wade made a profound statement that changed my life from that day forward. He said there was a preacher here and that God had said for him to cast his lot here. Before I knew it, I stood up, walked down the aisle, and sat in a chair with tears flowing down my face. Unbeknownst to me, God would knit Pastor Wade's spirit and my spirit together.

One Thursday my friend came to work and asked me whether I knew Rev. Wade had died last night. I told him no. We went together to the church to view Rev. Wade's body. As I walked down the aisle, I saw his body in a Shepherd's casket, fully displayed. I was stunned. Pastor Wade had on a brown suit and brown shoes. I had on a brown suit and the same brown shoes. At this time I didn't understand the significance.

Life Changing News

The news of his death moved me, and I changed my life's schedule. I gave up playing sports and dedicated myself to church functions. The church had approximately five other associate preachers, including the former pastor's son. In my opinion, one of the associates had a very strong preaching gift. He was my choice to succeed Pastor Wade. However, after the funeral the preacher became ill. He was hospitalized due to the illness. After he recovered enough to be released, I picked him up and took him home. On that day he collapsed in the lobby as we were leaving and unfortunately passed away that day.

I was led by the Holy Spirit to take a more active role in leadership at the church during the search for a new pastor. I began showing up to all the programs. At that time the church had five services: 8:00 a.m., 9:00 a.m., 11:00 a.m., 3:00 p.m., and 7:00 p.m. I was faithful to every one of those services and I heard one member say, "That little preacher is like an old shoe. When you don't have anything else, it's the most comfortable thing to put on." I didn't understand the significance of that statement, but as the church searched for a new pastor, I learned what it meant to be faithful.

To my count, 229 applicants applied to the church. The deacons called a meeting to elect a new pastor from the final four candidates. They choose the past moderator of the District Association to run the meeting. The deacons didn't want the present moderator to moderate the meeting, as they had candidates from Toledo, Ohio; Austin, Texas; and Battle Creek, Michigan, in mind. I was not their choice. The deacons had an influential relationship with the previous moderator and chose to use him for the election meeting. Not to mention, the former moderator also had a candidate of choice in the running. He was not for me. Some years later a new moderator was elected, Pastor William Wyne. He would use his influence to bring the President of the National Baptist Convention, USA to Lily Missionary Baptist Church to preach in October 2016. Significantly, this was the first time the National President, Jerry Young, had ever been in the State of Michigan. God is an amazing orchestrator. What some meant for evil, God meant for good.

Vote

That night we voted for a pastor. Yes, I said "we." I had no intention of becoming the pastor. That night the vote got down to the final two candidates, the candidates from Battle Creek, Michigan; and Austin, Texas. I was voting for the preacher from Texas until one old mother, Mother Brown, asked the moderator whether they could nominate someone else. The moderator made the mistake by saying yes. Therefore, the floor was open, and the woman said, "We would like to nominate the boy preacher." At the time I didn't know they were talking about me, and the moderator said, "Anybody who is nominated needs a **résumé**."

Unbeknownst to me, there was a coworker at the utility company who had written a **résumé** for me and submitted it to the church. One of the deacons had my **résumé**, and he began reading it aloud. I discovered they were talking about me. I asked the moderator whether I could add something to the **résumé**. That night I wrote with a pen, saying that I wasn't married, that I'd been with one woman, my wife, all my life, and that I did what married folks do. I thought this transparent revelation would sabotage my candidacy, but God had His way.

As I stated, God had His way. One of the older deacons asked the younger deacon, "Why didn't you read what he wrote?" So he grabbed the **résumé,** and he stated to the congregation, "This young man has been with one woman all of his life, and they do what married folk do. We should not vote a man in like that."

A church mother stood up and said, "He's been with one woman, but we can't say that about you guys." And that night the church stood up and voted me in as pastor in January 1988, and I was installed in March 1988.

Take Your Wife or Pastor His Wife

Sad to say, my life was in turmoil during my third year of pastoring the church and living my life. There was an uprising against me through some of the deacons and church leaders. Well, as God would have it, I had to call the current moderator to conduct a meeting where the issue was whether to retain me as pastor. They were taking a vote on whether to keep me or get rid of me. I will never forget what one of the associate preachers said that night. He said "Let's have a private vote so the people will not be against each other." However, the moderator disagreed. The moderator stated "Pastor Hines needs to know who's with him." So they registered all the voters. There were 669.

That night they began to read charges against me. One of the charges plainly said, "He has taken so many young people in this church that when we vote, it always comes out on his side, because all of the young people always vote with his ideas." Well, at that same instant it was sunny out, it began to lightning and thunder like never before. This might sound somewhat fishy, but the truth is, lightning hit the church as they were reading the charges against me. It knocked the lights out and the deacon kept reading in the dark. When he finished with the charges, the lights came back on.

The church took a vote that night. There were 660 for and nine against. Nine included five deacons, the choir director, and a couple of older members. The following day, on Sunday morning, God led me to walk into the pulpit. The subject was the story of Sampson—"When a weak man becomes strong"—out of the book of Judges. In that sermon I stopped, turned toward the deacons, and made a statement I will always live with for the rest of my life. I said to them "God said, 'If you don't let me pastor His wife, he's going to take your wife.'"

Within five months three deacons' wives died, and the fourth deacon's wife had one of her legs cut off. She begged her husband to get me and bring me to the hospital so she could beg me for forgiveness. That woman lived another ten years, always being a testimony of "Don't fight the preacher."

There was one deacon who was convinced to fight me to the end. His first wife died. He remarried and his second wife also died. He remarried third time and she had a massive stroke, but she survived. She divorced the deacon and moved out of state. I saw her in my favorite restaurant some ten years later. She was doing well.

As God would have it, I coached a young man in track and field in my home town of Benton Harbor, Michigan. This young man became a significant piece in the healing process between the deacon and me. It turned out that the young man was the deacon's grandson, but due to life circumstances, had never met. When I discovered the relationship, I made it a point to connect them. Both the grandfather and his grandson were glad to meet each other. During this meeting, the deacon and I shook hands and became friends. He died soon after that. I learned to live in harmony with others during my season of affliction.

The Mystery concerning the Church

"Be ye therefore followers of God, as dear children." When the saints learn how to have harmony, they can have progress. That was one of the mysteries God taught me even during this difficult time of my life. While studying Ephesians, I learned about the three walks that brought me closer to harmony. Ephesians 5:2 says, "Walk in love as Christ has also has loved us." In other words, walk with a spirit of sacrifice. The second walk is found in Ephesians 5:8, which says, "Walk as children of light." This verse teaches us that the Word sanctifies us.

We discover the third walk in 5:13, where Paul says, "Walk circumspectly"—or, in other words, walk wisely. When we master the three walks, verse 16 will come alive. Verses 17 and 18 indicate that we should understand God's will for our life, which is to be Spirit filled. Verses 19–21 teach us how to be Spirit filled. Then you will learn to submit yourselves one to another.

I call your attention to submitting; sometimes that is an ugly word when it is applied only in verse 22. But submitting to God isn't the *order* of authority but what *governs* authority. That is what Jesus said to the disciples when they were having a discussion. "Master, who is the greatest in the Kingdom of heaven?" And He said in Matthew 18:4, "Except your humble yourself and become as a little child, you will not otherwise enter the kingdom of heaven."

The Story Gets Out

On March 22, 1999, a local news reporter wrote a story about a pastor giving his life savings away to better his flock, which entailed building a new church and center. The center would be called the Lily Mission Center under the umbrella of the church. The article brought much attention to the movement of God. As a result of the article, I received many letters of support and contributions toward the project. It is significant to mention that the first letter I received included a check in the amount of $200 and some powerful words that proved to be prophetic. The writer said, "Watch God supply the need." I had $50,000 in cash and we needed $490,000 to purchase property for the building project, but God was in the business of taking two fish and five loaves, and feeding the multitude. I believed God for provision. The church had a parking lot consisting of three city lots on a quarter of an acre. The local hospital offered $35,000 for the lots. The church trustees wanted $40,000. I asked them whether I could negotiate the deal with the understanding that whatever I got over the $40,000 could be used to build the new church and center.

I went to the hospital, met the treasurer, and asked him the same question I always ask people. "Where are you from?" He said, "Kalamazoo, Michigan."

He was a tall man, and I asked him whether he played basketball.

He said yes, and I told him I had played for the legendary Benton Harbor Tigers. We began to build our relationship, and he shared with me that the president thought I was unusual. She had never met anyone who would sacrifice so much for people he or she barely knew. She had read the article Monetta Harr wrote about me. She made an offer I could not refuse. Their first offer was half a million dollars for the city lots. I hadn't taken the business class in negotiating. Never take the first offer. So I took the half a million and paid the land owners their $490,000. Over the course of three years, I received more letters and conducted a fund raising event. It is amazing to note that contributions from 24 of the letters coupled with the one fund raising event totaled $1,693, 145!

The Cutting of Trees

I had two acres of woods and condemned buildings on the site where the new church was being built, directly behind the old church. I could not see the streets on either side. Garbage was waist high. I had met a contractor out of Ohio who agreed to build the church for $5 million. I asked hospital officials whether they would assist me in talking with a local bank to lend me the $5 million. The bank agreed to lend me $2.5 million if I could raise $2.5 million.

What I had thought was somewhat difficult became a great miracle. Part of the construction was $150,000 to clear the land. Hoping to cut the fat out of the budget, I bought an ax and a saw and began to cut down trees and tear down homes myself. I worked approximately 14 hours a day for 26 days clearing trees and houses. On Sunday, I would preach, change my robe, put on my work clothes, and go out the back of the church into the woods. I cut trees as church members drove by and wondered what in the world was I doing. God was bringing about a miracle.

There was one man who drove a local truck for a delivery company, and he would drive by while eating his lunch and watch me. One day he said to me, "Do you need any help?"

I did not respond to him, because I did not have time to stop. On his own volition, he came out and joined me in the evenings Monday through Thursday. He took off work every Friday giving up $500 of pay per week to help me cut the trees. He was living with his girlfriend and their three children at the time. During our time cutting trees, I ministered to him about being married and giving everybody in the house his last name. We eventually cleared the land. He married the young lady, sent all three of his children to college, and eventually became a trustee at the Lily Missionary Baptist Church. He was saved and baptized during the year of clearing the trees. God gave me a vision to add a center that would carry out the mission of the church in blessing the community.

One Miracle Right after Another

The first miracle was for me, not for the congregation. As I lay prostrate in the old church praying about the building project, I asked God for a sign that this was His will and not simply my desire. Within minutes of that prayer, God sent a man by the name of Chuck to the church. I had never seen or met Chuck before. However, he said, "God had instructed him to find me and that he had been looking for me for weeks." He placed a roll of $100 bills in my hand totaling $10,000. This fueled my belief to move forward with the project. I used some of the money to purchase saws and axes and began to clear the land, which encompassed two acres.

In the process of clearing the trees, two trustees from a community foundation approached me. They had read the article about my wife and me giving the $50,000. It caused them to request a lunch with me, and they stated the community foundation would like to give me $75,000 toward the project. A week later a person who I did not know gave me a check for $20,000. This person encouraged me to keep working, stating that the project wasn't just my project, but all the community's project. The statement was verified when a man from a local company agreed to give me $25,000 over five years and committed his son's business for another $25,000. On another occasion while I was in the woods, a man approached me and asked me to go to lunch with him. I was somewhat hesitant, but I put down my tools and rode with him to lunch. We had lunch, and he gave me a check for $35,000 toward the building of the Lily Mission Center project. The center was created as 501(c)(3) Faith-based entity. It was a faith-based approach to help improve outcomes for "at risk" youth who the traditional human services system may have failed. The center welcomes and serves individuals regardless of religious beliefs or affiliation.

I met the man a month later and talked about the financial strain the project was under. He committed $300,000 over the next three years. This man later became a great friend, known as "Mr. Tony," in the words of my children. That was $100,000 a year for three years. Later, as the land was cleared, we set up for groundbreaking. United Way came on board and contributed $100,000 toward the Lily Mission Center's After School Program. The school superintendents of Jackson County at the time came together and proposed to use the Lily Mission Center to work with children that had been expelled from school. They were to pay $7,000 per month to use 20,000 square feet of the building. The health department put up $250,000 for our teen pregnancy ministry. Herbalife came to make us healthy with over $100,000 to help us to finish what we started.

Bank Reneges, but a miracle takes place

During the ground breaking celebration, a man asked me to meet with him. He was the trustee of a local foundation. I didn't know what God was exposing me to, but I remembered the words of my late father, the Reverend Joe Hines. He told me to get an older man to mentor me. This man became that mentor. Upon our introduction, I called him "Dad" and did so from that day forward. About our third meeting, he asked me what was on my mind, and I told him that the bank had reneged on its promise to loan the church $2.5 million and that I had spent $1 million in the building foundation. I needed $200,000 to continue the work, as the contractors were going to stop working the next day because I was $187,000 behind in payments to them. He asked me who else at the church was involved in the project. I told him there were five other men at the church working with me on the project. I fondly named them, "The Jackson 5."

Dad scheduled another meeting with me and the other men and asked questions about the building project and accountability. I explained to him that I was a man of faith and that I was working my faith. He walked out of the room and came back about ten minutes later committing $500,000 to the building project over three years. He asked me to join him in a meeting with the bank president. I told him the bank was closed. He called the bank president and told him to open the bank. We met the bank president at his office. He said to the bank president, "Pastor Hines needs $187,000 wired tonight to keep contractors working." The president of the bank said to him that Pastor Hines needed more collateral. Larry produced a letter guaranteeing that over the course of three years he would give me $500,000. He gave a check for $200,000 that day, and the bank president wired the construction company a payment for $187,000, and the bank released the other $2.5 million. To God be the glory; this was a very dramatic moment for me and the start of many miracles to come.

Miracles Forthcoming

The very next day, I had a visit from my neighbor, a beautiful little lady of faith. She rang my doorbell. I opened the door and greeted her. She said, "I don't want to take up much of your time, but here is an envelope." I took the envelope, sat down and opened it. In it was a cashier's check for $25,000 with a note on it that said, "You walk the talk." I knew then that God had done a miracle outside the church, and I was waiting for God to do a miracle inside the church.

Every Sunday I stood at the pulpit and said, "Brother so-and-so has given me a check for five thousand dollars, ten thousands dollar, twenty-five thousand dollars, and one hundred thousand dollars to help pay for the five-million-dollar structure." It appeared to me that the community had caught the vision, but the congregation had not. The miracles God was doing on the outside to change the church on the inside did not seem to move the church. I knew then that God would have to move in the people to change their minds about giving. The congregation did not jump aboard as quickly as I had hoped. But, as Moses told the new generation of Israel that God would deliver them little by little, Deuteronomy 7:20-22. I saw God change the hearts of the congregation. As their hearts changed, their hands gave.

Developing a Different Saint

I worked toward raising a new Israel through educating the younger congregation as well as the old about finance. I challenged young people in my church to save $2.74 a day; at the end of one year, I would match them. They would have a total of $1,010, and I would give them $1,000. The congregants began to catch fire to the challenge, and I formulated what I call the "$1,000 Club" and the "$10,000 Club." I began to encourage the young saints to take charge of their finances and to become givers in the work of God. I later insisted that the contractor would hire young people from my church since I was giving him $5 million. I knew he could find some kind of work for them to do.

Eventually he hired some of the young people from my church. I knew it would build a testimony in them that they had helped build the church from the ground up. Warren is one of the young men who received the $1,000 matching gift and worked on the church from the ground up. Today Warren is a deacon and trustee at the Lily Missionary Baptist Church. He is an officer of the law. Robert is another young man who worked for the contractor. He no longer lives in Jackson, Michigan. He is married and has a daughter name Lily.

Building a Church within a Structure

Building a financial structure in the church takes deliverance and discipleship. Some things are taught, as Jesus said in John 5:19. "I do as my Father does." I knew I must become transparent to the congregation so they could pick up the spirit of giving. So I began to take young people aside and sign them up for retirement accounts. I would give them their first $250 to open a brokerage account and then encourage them to save. I challenged them to stop living with their girlfriends and get married. This advice became a joke in town: "If you want a husband or a wife, go to the Lily Missionary Baptist Church."

I had to give up my resources to assure them it was the right thing to do. I began to give $1,000 to young people in my church who would get married. I had one drummer who I knew had to get married. He had a son with a young lady to whom he was not married. He was active in the ministry and it was important that his life aligned with the ministry. I cut my salary and encouraged the church to pay the difference to the drummer. I encouraged him to put it in a mutual fund and not spend it. He became one of the foundational blocks in the $10,000 Club. His father was an associate preacher in the church, and his mother was a very caring woman in the church. I pushed him openly in public by stopping in the middle of my sermon and saying, "Marry that young woman." He eventually married her and had another child. She was a great help to him in finishing his college degree. He applied for the state trooper Class of 2013, while working at a youth facility in Albion, Michigan. I took him to get his first uniform for trooper school, and began talking to him about commitment and dedication to his wife. He eventually passed trooper school and now is employed as a state trooper for the state of Michigan.

I encouraged building wealth; it was a sensitive issue in the congregation. I would always ask the people, "How are your finances and how is your relationship with God?" I learned one part of that from the late Pastor A.P. Williams, who was a pastor for fifty-plus years in our city. People became uneasy with my asking and encouraging them about their savings and bill-paying habits.

Word Impacts Wealth

As I was returning from a missionary trip in Detroit, Michigan, I asked one of my members, a young school teacher, "Are you in a savings plan?" She replied, "I'm not able to save at this time." I challenged her that if she would save one hundred dollars, I would give her one hundred dollars. She eventually mastered saving, and I challenged her to apply the Word of God to her life pertaining to financial stewardship. She became one of the leading teachers in the Word of Wealth, a portion of the morning worship where we educate the congregation about finance according to the word of God. Every Sunday you would hear some inspired Word of God about saving. Our platform for this Word of Wealth ministry was Psalms 37 and 12. The wicked borrow and don't pay back. We couldn't be the salt of the earth and a city on a hill if we didn't pay our bills. Our testimony was condemning our God. And so I encouraged the saints to bring one bill in and put it on the cross located in the sanctuary. When the bill was paid off, they took the bill down and worked on paying another bill. It was the pile of victory. The church offering grew though the congregation was getting smaller.

Growing in the Church and in Marriage

It's a mystery, I tell you. As I grew in Lily Baptist, I grew in my marriage. As I learned to change and submit to my wife, I learned how to submit myself to the saints of God in the church. I was to be an example to them in sacrifice, in life, or in light and in wisdom. Many things transpired.

With that being said, when I first took over as pastor of Lily Missionary Baptist Church, Lily Baptist was a good church. However, its stewardship was questionable. The people had substituted God's plan with their own. God has asked us to be tithers and givers, and Lily Baptist had instituted selling in the church. I don't know what your view on selling is, but according to John 2:16, when they were selling in the temple, Jesus drove the sellers out and said, "Take these things hence; make not my Father's house an house of merchandise."

That was the platform I was using after my second year, when I asked Lily Baptist not to have their Rose Tea. It was the biggest-selling project in the church ministry. It was where they made baked goods and dinners, and sold them. They produced rose gardens, and people would come and buy roses. I asked them, "How much money did you profit from the Rose Tea?" They told me the profit of about $1,800 was the most they had ever made. I asked them not to sell and only take donations. If they didn't make the profit of $1,800, I would give them

$2,000. Well, at the end of that donation drive, I asked them, "How much did you profit?" The process took them a couple of weeks, and they responded back to me, "$3,000."

So I encouraged them not to sell products anymore, and they told me that if they couldn't do the Rose Tea the way they had always done it, they didn't want to do it. To this day, Lily Missionary Baptist Church no longer has a Rose Tea. That was one of the stepping stones in stopping the church from lying. They changed the word from *selling* to *donation* and set a price, and I told them a donation was whatever people wanted to give, not a price someone set.

I eventually started to give away food and drinks to the public for free. I invaded Jackson High School in Jackson, Michigan. They had an annual track meet called Selby's Track Meet, which invited all the best athletes from around the county. About 18 high schools participated. I went to the high school athletic director, who was an associate preacher at the Lily Missionary Baptist Church, and asked him whether I could give away free food to participants and parents. At the time I took $5,000 from me and Sister Hines's wealth. This purchased all meat and drinks, and I asked the young congregation to donate side dishes. The event grew from feeding 500 people to nearly 3,000. They came from all around, in the month of May, to eat for free. We were known for several things, everything from salmon to chicken, and barbecue ribs to sweet potato pies and salmon salad.

This charity called the church to be known in the community. It wasn't the preaching or singing that eventually got into the hearts and minds of the people in the community. It was the work of Christ that touched the community. But there was still work to be done in the church itself concerning the spirit of giving. The church took in about $500 each Sunday. In my first pastoral year, the old church still had a debt of $67,000 left on the $100,000 loan at a local bank, which was charging 12 percent interest.

I went to the older saints of the church and asked them to contribute all their change. I got some very trustworthy trustees, and we drove to each of the members' houses, collected change, went to the local bank, and paid right on the mortgage. In 1989, my second year, the mortgage was paid in full. The next step was to get the church to live on a budget.

My first meeting was to try to educate them that a budget wasn't concrete; it was flexible. This part led to some challenges, as I wanted to update the church from handwritten to computerized technology. I can remember that first announcement that I needed 12 members to contribute $100 to purchase our first computer. I remember one of the deacons telling me I would never get the money. One lady, who has since gone home to be with the Lord, wrote the check for $1,200. She delivered the "bacon," and we purchased the first church computer. I began to give them an accurate record of expenditures and money collected. I began including what everybody had given the past Sunday in the morning bulletins. People were somewhat taken aback, but the situation began to settle with the people, and still to this day we now print out a quarterly report at our first Sunday fellowship.

I changed the time of our business meetings. There were originally held on Saturday evenings. I scheduled them for Saturday morning. The meetings seem to foster frustration in the evenings, which carried over to Sunday morning worship. When I changed the meeting to Saturday mornings, the crowd went down, but the spirit went up. I can remember one member telling me she didn't like the Saturday morning meeting, and I said it was peaceful; there was no bickering. She said they enjoyed fighting with each other. I knew I had my work cut out for me.

I began to expose the church to a whole new order of preaching and teaching, worshipping, and giving. I selected my preachers and teachers based on their gifts and lifestyles. I knew this step would have a great benefit to the body of Christ or kingdom work.

Calling Things as though They Were

I began to speak to the church on Sunday morning with the revelation that things were already there. For example, I spoke as though the new baby grand piano, the new church building, and the center were already there. I saw people rejoicing to come to church. Eventually, all of the above came to pass. I began to have a transformation in the church from a programming church to a tithing church. I first had to expose myself to the good things tithing could bring about. I went to a funeral at a Catholic Church, took a slogan from the Catholic Church, and instituted it in my Protestant church. We do it every Sunday morning now—we hold our offering up, and people repeat after me: "Stewardship is what we do after we say, 'I believe.'" I saw that slogan in the Catholic Church and brought it to the Lily Missionary Baptist Church.

I began to bring in different evangelists, who exposed the church to a different way of preaching and teaching. One of my first evangelists was the late Reverend Jerome Kirby. He was a preacher of what I consider great ability. We began to trade pulpits, and this gave me a chance to expose my church to another level of how a church should take care of a pastor and his family.

In the old church building, we would invite guests, and the pastor and his guest would have to sit wherever there was an open seat. On this particular Sunday, we visited a church in Detroit, Michigan, and we were having dinner. They refused to let me sit down just anywhere. They had a "head table," and my wife and I sat with the late Pastor Jerome Kirby as his distinguished guests. When we got back to Jackson, Michigan, the sisterhood went to work. The next time we had a program, we had a head table, which is now called the "first family table." There were no longer paper cups, but there were silverware, glasses, and plates.

God eventually touched me to touch others in how to change ministry, especially in giving. Pastors would come and start the offering off with $25. I would start the offering off with $1,000. This giving took a lot of my resources, but as God would have it, I never went without. I began to sow into the pastors' children when they would come and run revival for me. I would take an offering not only for them, but also for their children. When their wives came, I would make sure we always had a gift for them. When they didn't come, I would always send a gift to them and a message that we'd missed their presence. I believe the pastor's wife gives the fragrance of the church. If she has a bad attitude, the church will have a bad attitude.

Down through the years, I've seen the giving of preachers change. I've always been bothered when I hear the teaching and preaching of sowing. I never saw the leaders sow, but they always requested the people to sow. So God led me to sow into the people. One New Year's evening I preached and the people took up an offering. It was passed around and I told people to take what they needed.

I remember one man who joined my church because he was in the audience on New Year's Eve. The church had taken up a large offering for me, and I instructed the ushers to pass the offering around and let the audience take what they needed. One of the people in the audience was a former professional basketball player. He had grown up in the projects and had been born poor most of his life. By his testimony, he had seen the church take advantage of his poor family. But this demonstration of selflessness touched him. I don't know what touches people or changes them, but God knows. The Spirit of God just led and directed me in this activity. It caused him to give his life to God.

The Beginning of the New Church

When I called the bishop to run the revival, he was from the Church of God and Christ. But he had fallen in the Church of God in Christ. His fall was due to drugs and now he was no longer appointed bishop of the Church of God and Christ. I met him through his brother-in-law, who pastored in the city. I wanted to give him a new start and encourage him in his gift, so I called him to run a revival at the Lily Missionary Baptist Church. During that week of revival, we decided to build our new church across the street. The bishop knew nothing about this, and he began to use his gift of healing and prophecy.

He said there was a person in the church whose feet were swollen and that God would reduce that swelling right now. I eventually told the congregation that night that I was the person in need. He also laid hands on one of my members who always came to church to prove the preacher was a fake. He hadn't worked in thirty years because he had back problems. That morning he called me to his house with tears in his eyes and told me his back no longer hurt he was healed. But during that service, the bishop said two things. He said, "I see a new church on the same block," and he prophesied that a brother would be a devoted help to me. That brother attended church but not like after that statement. To this day, he is one of the most faithful men in the church work. In my estimation, we could afford to pay one million dollars to build the church and center. But, God convinced me to build something we could not pay for so that when it is paid off we know God did it.

Circle of Leadership

Expanding the circle of leadership was a crucial and essential part of the development of Lily Missionary Baptist Church. I quickly installed the first woman trustee in the history of the Lily Missionary Baptist Church. As Deuteronomy 1:15 says, "So I took the leaders of your tribe wise and reputable individuals and installed them as leaders over you." I had to find people with gifts and integrity and sometimes that put people in position who were afraid of the responsibility. But I supplied the training and encouragement. In expanding this circle of leadership, I selected about five women and seven men to what I considered strengthening and building a church from the inside out. I first started with what I called the "new converts class." They thought the class was just about teaching Scripture, but it was intended to build leaders out of them.

I eventually selected individuals to be over the treasury, land acquisition, blueprint plans, and negotiations. I also selected an ambassador, a critical position whose mission was to keep the people from being afraid. I believed my task was to get my story told before someone else told the story. I'm of the mind-set that history is only "His story." So as we moved forward, we met once a week, and I gave what I call the "why." The why to me is the motivation that causes people to achieve. If your why is greater than your problem, you will be successful. I taught them that if they really wanted something to come to pass, God would supply the resources if we supplied the energy and faith. I knew God had already given us the resources and had, as Paul said, "much people in this city."

Developing the Saints

I had to seek out the saints who were poor or in need. I believed in Proverbs 22:9. He who has a bountiful life shall be blessed, for he gave of his bread to the poor. I remember one of my members losing his job after thirty years. He was working on a house putting shingles on with a hammer and nails. I asked him how long that would take. He said about two weeks. I asked him whether he had any other jobs. He said he had three other jobs lined up, but they would have to wait. I went to Sears and bought an air gun. I brought it back to him and told him, "Hurry up and get those other three jobs done."

I had another member who lost his job; he started to haul garbage, but his truck broke down. I gave him my truck and told him to make a living. These are just some of the examples God put in my life to change people's lives. The people who were touched eventually became some of the most faithful members in the church. I think I'm more blessed with caring members than with a bank full of money. Building a church isn't always about wood and nails but rather about love and kindness.

I eventually moved children from my congregation into my home to give them a chance in life. Three of the young men were saved during the revival week. I eventually had 32 young men live in my home. I am of the mind-set that all seeds blossom, but not at the same time.

I remember one child in my home that didn't fit into my personal rule of the house: nobody over 18. One Sunday some of the children had evangelized and brought another child to church, who was living in an abandoned house. I didn't know that fact at the time, but as he sat in the back of my church, I said to him, "God said for you to come and live with me." He didn't immediately take me up on this offer. He eventually showed up at my house during the winter months. The house he was living in had no heat. He was over 18, but God had spoken to me to take this young man in and give him a chance. I told him that he needed a job and must go back to school. He told me he didn't have any money. So I took my credit card and enrolled him in Jackson Community College.

He loved going to Western Michigan University every other weekend to visit his cousin, who'd brought him to the Lily Missionary Baptist Church; His cousin was another young man I had worked with in the past. I told him that if he liked Western Michigan University that much, he should go there. He said to me that he didn't think he could get in. I advised him to call the counselor and ask him what classes and grades he needed to have to get into Western. The process took the young man a year, and he ended up with a 4.0 grade point average at Jackson Community College. Then he was accepted at Western Michigan University.

He attended Western Michigan University and got a young girl pregnant. I instructed him that he needed to marry that young girl. He married her and graduated from Western Michigan University. He and his wife got jobs in the Grand Rapids public schools. Some years later, he received his master's degree from Grand Valley State University. While living with me this same young man helped me cut down the trees and clear the land where Lily Missionary Baptist Church now sits.

Those are just some of the people God has allowed me to work with—and to be worked on. Every time I tell his story, it brings tears to my heart, because here was a man I had no room for because of a rule I'd created. But the voice of God created room in my heart and home. Now this young man is a father of two and a happily married man.

God's People Already in Place

Many blessed people have come into my life to help shape my belief in God and to know Him better. Besides the children who lived in my house, there was one young man by the name of Clyde Robinson who I met while I was in my first year here in Jackson. He was a also a program analyst. Clyde, a native of Louisiana, came from a very poor background.

Clyde eventually became an active member at Lily Missionary Baptist Church. He became a deacon under me. Clyde was married with one child at the time. He eventually left the company and went to work for a company in Lansing, Michigan. This is how I came to work in Lansing. As I was serving as pastor of Lily Missionary Baptist Church for $125 a week, I was laid off from the utility company for which I was working due to a downsizingin May 1991. They gave me a compensation package that paid me six months' salary. Clyde thought I was going to leave Lily Missionary Baptist Church to seek better employment, and he was correct.

A couple of churches that had heard me preach in the state of Georgia had begun to recruit me and solicit my gift to become their pastor. I had offers from $100,000 a year with a housing and car allowance. These were very enticing to me as I contemplated moving south to be able to preach and live. I shared this news with Clyde Robinson, and, unbeknownst to me, he went to work at his job to secure employment for me. The company was in a hiring freeze, and he asked the president if they would give his job to his pastor if he quit. The president thought the request showed such a great spirit, so they agreed to it.

Clyde called me and asked me to apply. Within a week, I was given a call. I was hired, and I had Clyde's desk. His family photo was still on the desk. The answering machine still had his voice. I didn't really understand what was going on, but later I found out that Clyde had quit with the understanding that they would hire me in his place. I remind you that my wife was working, and Clyde was the sole breadwinner in his family. His wife, Pat, worked some part-time jobs, but basically she was a homemaker. They had one child, and she was pregnant. Clyde wasn't able to receive unemployment because he quit his job.

A company in Battle Creek, Michigan, eventually hired Clyde as a program analyst. Clyde drove 45 miles a day one way to go to work. He eventually moved to Battle Creek. A couple of years later, when his oldest son was a sophomore, Clyde received a promotion to work in one of the distribution centers in Memphis, Tennessee. Clyde had always had a desire to take his wife Pat back south to be close to their parents. One of Pat's parents died when they were in Memphis.

I had always promised Clyde I would come and see his son play basketball before he finished high school. I eventually went during Brandon's senior year and saw him play. Clyde eventually received another promotion to work at a distribution center in Oklahoma. Both of Clyde's parents eventually died. As I was writing this book, I called Clyde on May 9, and he said to me, "Reverend, I was glad to show up for your 25th pastoral celebration." They had snuck Clyde back in town. I hadn't seen him in ten years, and he was the emcee of my 25th pastoral appreciation.

Clyde shared with me over the phone that he'd received another promotion and that he was going to run the distribution center in his home state of Louisiana. He had finally made it back home. I say all this to say that I watched God be faithful to Clyde, because Clyde had really given of himself to me. Clyde took a step of faith by walking off a job to secure a pastor for the people. He wasn't the typical spiritual church worker, but he had plenty of wisdom, love, and care for the pastor and young people in the church. He had a passion like I did.

Clyde actually helped me start a care package ministry for kids who went to college. We would send boxes of cornflakes, a roll of quarters, and a copy of what Clyde called the "top four sermons of the month." I always promised kids from the church if they went to college, I would go to class with them one day before they graduated. During that visit, lunch would be on me. At the time most of the children went to Michigan, Michigan State, Western Michigan, Central Michigan, or Eastern Michigan. That was an easy trip.

But I had two twins Clyde helped get into Southern University in Louisiana. When they were seniors we made the trip to Louisiana. It took us about 18 hours. I got in touch with one of the twins' professors and asked whether I could sit in the class and surprise the young man. I stated that I was his pastor from up north and that I had promised I would attend a class with them before they graduated. The professor accepted the invitation, and I was the guest for the day. Both of the twins graduated from college. One is a trustee at Lily, and the other one is a school teacher in Louisiana.

Clyde was a great source of encouragement, commitment, and "stick-to-it-ness." He probably couldn't sing in tune to a hymn, but he could work as unto the Lord. He is one of the truly great friends I've ever had in the work of God.

Private Problems Become Public

As I mentioned earlier, God's people are in place. God had strategically placed one of my good friends, "the Reverend," in my life and in the congregation. We called his son, l "Little Reverend." He led the Reverend to the church. The Reverend became an ambassador for the church, and he connected me with people who were renowned. I began to use these contacts, bringing them on site to bring awareness to children who were in trouble. One of them was a famous football coach who did a fundraiser one night; about 350 people showed up, and we raised $103,000. God placed the Reverend in our presence so we could meet and build relationships with these individuals. Many of them participated in the "Men of Valor" camp, where we would bring professional athletes in to talk about self-discipline and the role it plays in success.

But sometimes people's private problems come to light to destroy the light. One evening, the Reverend, when he was driving from the grocery store, was pulled over and arrested for a DUI (driving under the influence). Now, remember the Reverend is a preacher in the church. I received a phone call informing me of the situation. I used my influence to guide the Reverend's situation under the radar. But I had a prominent member who insisted on exposing the Reverend. He informed the newspaper and police department about the situation. That night I picked the Reverend up from the police department and encouraged him to come to church Sunday morning.

I knew the situation was hard for him, but I had to tell the church so that the Devil wouldn't be glorified. I understand restoring one in meekness, but the Sunday morning paper had his picture on the front page. I had him stand up in the church, and I told the church if any of my children went to jail, I will go down and get them out.

I sat the Reverend down for 60 days. He must attend every service and not take part in any leadership. I was keeping the standard of the church high but applying what I call "a man needs a hand" when he is sinking.

Remember when Peter was walking on water and started to sink? Jesus didn't ask him anything; He just gave him a hand. Private problems can become public, but we can turn them into glory for God. I had a member who was an usher; his business was raided, and cocaine was found. He was on the front page of the paper and didn't show up at church. During the morning service, right before I began to preach, I took out my cell phone at the altar, called him, put him on the speaker, and had the church say, "We love you and miss you." He returned to church the next Sunday. I publicly told him he could no longer serve in the capacity as an usher until notified, but he could always serve as a fallen saint who has gotten up. These are some private problems that become public; we must deal with them to help people.

CHAPTER 3

Finances

Let me say that God was the first to change my heart and mind about my finances. God also worked a miracle in changing the hearts of the saints whom I pastor, and He did a miracle in the minds of the people in the community. God taught me to appreciate working and saving. I began to save some money in an aluminum can. Eventually, every December I went to the local bank and bought a certificate of deposit.

As I nurtured and observed the church, I noticed couples who made more money than my wife and I did, but they never seemed to *have* more money than we had. They had the appearance of wealth, but they never had the actual substance. They were God's people, but as a servant of God, I noticed they were always financially hungry.

Schemes and gadgets were very common among the congregation. Wolves in sheep's clothing could very easily enter the fold. From pyramid schemes to lottery tickets to horse racing to any type of get-rich-quick scheme, financial troubles seemed to attach or latch on to the saints of God. I knew God had sent wealth to the congregation, but the congregation lived in the spiritual realm of being unable to financially support Kingdom work. It was my assignment to show them God had provided enough. Discipline, or the lack thereof, was the problem.

Deliverance and Discipleship

I began to minister in the areas of deliverance and discipleship. In some churches, mainly in the Church of God in Christ, they concentrate heavily on the spirit of deliverance. In Presbyterian and Baptist churches, they concentrate heavily on discipleship. I met these two spirits by fellowshipping with my wife's family. Her father was from the Church of God in Christ, and her mother was from the Presbyterian Church. My wife attended a local Baptist church while she was in high school. God was preparing her for the work He'd assigned to my hands.

I quickly learned to aspire to these concepts. As Ruth said to Naomi, "Thy people shall be my people and thy God my God" (Ruth 1:16c). A move of God began to take place in the congregation of the saints. They began tithing and obeying the direction that God has given me.

I implemented a plan of discipleship by bringing them to my home two-by-two for personal discussion and enlightenment.

I was transparent with two couples. They were both living in apartments, and my wife and I were living in a $125,000 house. The wives worked together at the same company, and both husbands worked for the local school district. I estimated their household income in the 1990s to be approximately $100,000 apiece. They were living in apartments, which cost them about $900 a month. Conversely, I paid a mortgage of $600 a month. They didn't participate in their company's saving plan, and they weren't building personal wealth on their own.

I began to slowly convince them to sign up for their 401(k) savings plan and save money in a can. Their testimonies grew from being able to pay for vacations out of the can and having their first down payment on their first homes in Jackson, Michigan. Couples one and two are both about five years older than me, and their children were teenagers, and my children preschoolers. In effort to impress upon them the need to plan ahead, I showed them banks accounts for my children that were opened before they were born. I was planning on having four children and God blessed me with two.

I showed the couples accounts where I had begun saving for everything including high school graduation open houses, college education, weddings, and to purchase their first homes. I put $2.74 a day away, allowing me to save a total of $1,010 a year. I invested in four different funds, mid-cap, growth, growth-income, and bond funds. Later, I moved to a brokerage firm.

Need for Atmosphere

I was inspired by God to move some of the funds to the brokerage firm so that my children could get exposure to saving and investing. When my children were small, every payday my wife took them grocery shopping with her. As a treat, or more so a bribe, she would always allow them to buy an ice cream cone, and ride the penny pony. I shared with her that our children needed to experience the savings and investing spirit, not the spending spirit. This was a revelation from God for my family and my church. As is stated in 1 Timothy 3:5, "For if a man know not how to rule his own house, how shall he take care of the church of God?" My children were being exposed only to spending money and never to saving it as so was the church family.

Over the years I taught my children what I called the "Hines giving, saving, and investing factor." Give and save in that order. Still today my children believe in giving, saving, and investing—in that order. A brokerage-firm atmosphere allowed me to instill in my children that they needed to grasp the concept of using money to bring about kingdom work. My wife quickly adopted this frame of mind and began to take my children to the credit union when she received her check and exposed them to saving instead of spending.

Personal Growth

As I followed the plan of giving, saving and investing, I developed more faith in trusting God with my finances. As He did with David, God developed my faith privately to use me publicly. Prior to his facing Goliath, David had experienced killing a lion and a bear privately. My private development came through my saving $36,000 in change in a can over the course of 12 years. The money was divided three ways. My daughter Alyse received one-third, my son, Joseph received a third and my wife and I received a third. This was the starting point of trusting God with my wealth. I had always tithed and given, but never to the point of obeying God with all. My love for God grew as I saw God take little and make much. Every December I took my can of change down to the bank with my children and bought certificates of deposits. By the time my daughter was six years old, her share was $11,000. At the same time period, My son's share was $13,000; he was eight years old. Twelve thousand belonged to my wife and me.

God spoke to my spirit, "Give it all to the church to build a new church." I wrestled with God—but to no avail. I asked godly people whether they would give away all they had at the urging of God's voice. Some said they would; others said they wouldn't. But every time someone said he or she would, it appeared as though I heard God's voice speaking to me. The last person I asked was my wife in the middle of the night. Her response changed my life forever. She told me with no hesitation, *"We came here poor, and we can leave here poor."* I think you need to understand the word *poor* in my wife's description. When I came to Jackson, Michigan, in June 1986, I had $282, a loan from my parents, which was all they had to give me. My father gave me a tool box, a very special gift that I still have and treasure today. My girlfriend at the time, Leontyne, bought me three white shirts and two pair of pants- a grey and a blue pair. I did not have much more than that when we were married on August 13, 1988.

Wealth and Faith

My rent was $240 a month. My wife had just graduated from Michigan State University. To say the least, she didn't have much in tangible wealth. As we saved our $36,000, we felt very wealthy. Nevertheless, in obedience to God, I went to the bank to withdraw the money to give it to the church at my 11th pastoral anniversary celebration. I was going to give the $36,000 to the church, as they were acknowledging me for being the pastor. They were having appreciation services at the church in my honor, which included giving me money as an expression of love. I heard God speak in my spirit, "listen to banker." While I was at the bank, a loan officer convinced me not to give all my money away, saying that, "Cash is king." I asked him what he meant. He said, "We will use your $36,000 as collateral to borrow $50,000."

I asked him what terms would be used. He said four percent on your $36,000 and six percent on the bank's $50,000. I took the $50,000 cashier's check. I went and purchased a life insurance policy that equaled a sum of $100,000. I wrote the policy beneficiaries to be Leontyne Hines ($50,000) and Lily Missionary Baptist Church ($50,000). I walked into the church that Sunday afternoon, and as they gave me $7,000, I gave them a $50,000 check and the policy of $100,000. I said to them, "God said, 'Build a new church.'" I took the $7,000 and secured two acres around the current church and asked each home buyer to write whatever amount he or she wanted for his or her home. The State Equalized Value (SEV) of five properties around the church was approximately $9,000 in appraisal, but people wrote $60,000 and $50,000 for their homes. The total bill for property came to $490,000.

I must say that God had told me five years before to buy the property when it was up for sale for back taxes of $19,000. At the time I proposed to the church to purchase the property. However, they voted no on the proposal. Ironically, some of the members of the church who voted no bought the property for themselves. I eventually had to buy the property from the members. There had to be a change of heart. They were God's people who did not share with the Kingdom work. But I remind you: I had $19,000, and God told *me* to buy the property, and I tried to pass off the responsibility to the church. This is the same thing Adam did in the Garden of Eden; he passed off responsibility on to Eve. (Gen. 3:12). I tried to pass off my responsibility to the church.

Today I'm trying to share with you what I call "destroying the generational curse." I have tried to leave my children with what I call uncommon faith, uncommon health, and uncommon wealth. I'm sharing with you how to put a stop to the curse and claim the promises of God. My father, the late Pastor Hines, would always say, "Pray like it depends on God and work like it depends on you." I've come up in a climate in which television and the local media have made African-Americans or people as a whole who are poor believe they must win the lottery or play in the NBA, NFL, or MLB to be able to pass substantial wealth on to their family. I'm going to try to dispel that spirit or belief by stating that you just need desire, self-discipline, and commitment. I will share with you about the wealth I'm passing on to my children in detail with a plan. As the Scripture says, where there is no vision, the people perish. As I stated earlier, I had called my children to my bedside and shared with them about the wealth I was leaving with them, and their responsibility was to guard the wealth. It is much easier for me to earn it, but it would take much more for them to guard it.

Detailed Plan

Psalm 90:12 says, "Lord, teach us to number our days."

1. I invested $10,000 I had built up over the years and looked for a 10 percent return. I instructed Joseph and Alyse that when Joseph was 32 and Alyse was 30, the amount should be $25,900. "Go buy a house and land." In my belief there is only so much land God ever made. Nobody else is making any more.

2. I set aside another $10,000, looking for a nine percent return, and instructed them that at their ages of 42 and 40, the amount should be $56,044, invest in a business. I believe that to become wealthy, you don't work for people; you have people work for you.

3. I invested another $10,000, looking for an annual nine percent return so that at their ages of 52 and 50, the amount should be $132,676. "Enjoy traveling. At that age you're wise enough to know what to do and what not to do, and if you aren't wise, ask God to give you wisdom."

4. I invested $6,500 and yearly would invest $1,200, looking for a 12 percent return. This amount would equal the sum of $1,082,825 at their ages of 59 and 57. I encouraged them to enjoy giving the money away. Remember what the Lord Jesus said; it is better to give than to receive.

5. Then I invested another $10,000 in a tax-free account that was paying four percent for their ages of 72and 70. "Enjoy inspiring others in kingdom work, in seed planting. Invest money in training people to know what God has given them to manage."

6. Finally, I invested $31,000, looking for a nine percent return for their ages of 72and 70. Fifty years later, this amount would be a sum of $2,230,725. "Pass the wealth on to the next generation instead of starting them off with $10,000." If each one of them had five children, I looked forward to having ten grandchildren. "Invest in our grandchildren's lives $100,000 apiece, just like their journey started." Lord, teach us to number our days.

Wisdom

To help people shatter the belief that you need a large sum to be able to break the generational curse of being poor, I'm going to share with you my tax filings. I kept all my tax filing from the year 1986. The most

I ever made in household income was $109,000. My wife and I came to this land that flowed with milk and honey with $18,500 annually apiece for a total of $37,000. That sum lasted until about the year 1992, when I received a job at MEA and was paid $45,000. In the year 1998, God led me to walk off my job. At the time the church was paying me $125 a week. Six months later a group of women gathered in my church and demanded a meeting with the officers of the church, asking the church to pay Pastor Hines a livable salary of $500 each Sunday. Thank God for women in the church. I was always told, "If you really want something done, seek out the sisterhood." I didn't seek them out; they just decided to do the right thing.

The Question

God has given me the wisdom to take two fish and five barley loaves, and feed multitudes. I always ask individuals a question: "How should a young man save his money?" God placed me in the presence of the Honorable President Bill Clinton, and in his presence I asked him that question. He shared with me how he had led the country out of debt: "Pay as you go." I had always applied this theory to my life. It was very confirming to my spirit to know I had placed myself as the covering of my family and church, and my mind-set was like the president of this great country.

And so I also placed myself in the spirit of the late Honorable President Franklin D. Roosevelt, who started social security to secure society. I had read up on the great President Roosevelt, so I decided to mimic his decision to secure the country. I was going to lead my family and church in the spirit of security. In 1998 Sister Hines and I gave the church $25,000 in stock to start the first investment through the brokerage firm. On the church's anniversary, we would try to model this stewardship by giving large sums of stock to the church to signify we had more than one pocket of giving. It wasn't based on the Friday paycheck. But we had other tangible wealth we were trying to awaken the congregation to. We displayed copies of stock certificates on the wall of the Investment Room in the church. Outside this room is a copy of a check from a U.S. General who wrote me to be part of the work God had assigned to my hands.

I want to encourage each and every one who reads this book that Solomon stated that money is the answer to all things. There is a spiritual war taking place to destroy the finances of the saints. We must be able to get control of our spending so we can do Kingdom work. So many saints believe they are saved and sanctified, filled with His precious holiness, yet they are bound by not paying debt. But the Scripture is true in Psalm 37:12; the wicked borrow and don't pay back. So I started to have special services to reduce debt, encouraging the saints to target the great devourer in their lives. I asked people to write down their smallest debt and pin it on the cross in the sanctuary to keep them focused on reducing their debt. When the debt was paid, they took it off the cross. They doubled up on the next payment to reduce that debt.

Therefore, I am pleading with you who read this book to get control of your finances. Pray for divine intervention so that you will have uncommon wealth. And when you master the favor of God, who promised He has given us power to make wealth Deut 8:18, you will see your health get better as worry and stress are relieved. When you recognize who gave you the wealth, you will have a mind-set to glorify Him in your giving. Where your treasure is, there is also your heart.

An Awakening from God

I believe God called me to give and be a model of giving. With commitment, sacrifice, and discipline you can accomplish growth in all the areas God has called you. It takes the Holy Spirit to achieve anything in God. Pray for the Holy Spirit to reveal God's plan for your life.

My life's journey started at the age of 12, when I knew God had called me to preach. I waited a decade later to confess my preaching to the public. After this persuasion in my life, I began to believe God for other things. When I was 14 years old, I asked God to let me marry Leontyne. She was in the seventh grade, and I was in the eighth grade. When my father was sick unto death at the age of 61, I went to his bedside. He assured me that God would let him live to be 78. My father died on April 4, 2001, and had turned 78 on March 23, 2001.

When God spoke to me in the middle of the night and told me to pastor the Lily Missionary Baptist Church in 1987 I was convinced. I believed God when He told me my wife would have children and that the first one would be a son. He told me to name him Joseph after my father. I believed and trusted God that He would bring my daughter, Alyse Angelica Hines, through her sickness. I am still persuaded that God will bring my son, Joseph, through his trials of life and help him discover his purpose in God. To this day I'm still convinced that God isn't a man that He should lie, according to Numbers 23:19. That's why I named this book *I Believed Him*.

CHAPTER 4

Family

Little Anointings

There's a reason I called this section the "little anointings." One day I sat in the audience of a Bill Cosby concert, and he walked up to me and said, "You look like a man who has little anointings." I accepted his words as something very special, and still to this day I have been blessed with anointed children. As I stated at the start of this book, there are four areas I want to share with you: finances, church, marriage, and now the fourth, family—which is mainly revelations about my children.

First, I want to talk about my son, Joseph. My wife and I tried to have children, but she wasn't getting pregnant. I asked one of the senior pastors in town about my problem, and he told me to lay my hands on my wife and pray. One night I got up in the middle of the night; as God's voice came to me, I began to pray. My wife got up and said, "Why did you hit me in the stomach?" That morning she went to the doctor. She later called home to inform me of her doctor's visit. At this point I was trying to deceive her that I was still employed. I wasn't supposed to be at the house to answer the phone. I was supposed to be at work. She told me she knew I was laid off, and she had good news—she was pregnant.

Well, as I mentioned about Clyde Robinson, I was laid off, and my last severance check from Consumers was scheduled to come November 11, 1991. The MEA hired me on November 4, 1991. My wife and I purchased our first home on December 27, 1991. My wife wanted to know where we were going to get the down payment, and I reminded her of the $25 we'd put away each month in a mutual fund in Kansas City. I made a call. They sent me a check for $16,000. Needless to say, God had put all the pieces together. I had proof of employment, I had a down payment, and my wife was pregnant. We had the closing on December 27, 1991, and the church family moved us in on January 11, 1992.

Joseph was born on that January 29, 1992. I will never forget it. What a great day. I always wanted a son named after me, but God had spoken to me and told me to name my son Joseph after my father, the late Reverend Joseph Hines. He was going to preach and accomplish great things. I knew Joseph was somewhat special, because I'd submitted to the will of God and didn't name him James. Up to now, I always tell Joseph, "Pray for a wife, honor God, and name your first son after your father." I used Joseph in lots of my revelation stories. People would insist that I would have comments at funerals or church programs if I wasn't the main speaker. One of the stories I told about Joseph was at a funeral.

A young girl's mother had been killed by her live-in boyfriend, and now her sister's boyfriend had tragically killed her. I went to the funeral because the young girl was a member of my church. My comment was about Joseph receiving his driver's license.

I told the story that I hadn't been confident that Joseph could drive as well as the instructor said he could. We were leaving the city of Jackson and heading to my hometown of Benton Harbor. A storm arose, a thundering storm. People were pulling over, but I kept telling Joseph to keep driving. He was afraid. Tears began to roll up in Joseph's eyes. I wouldn't let him pull over. We drove through that thunderous storm; when it let up, I told him to pull over.

He pulled over in amazement. "Why do you want me to stop now?"

I told him to get out of the car and look back. The storm was behind us, but all those people who had pulled over were still in the storm. I told the young lady at the funeral that there was a storm raging in her life. If you pull over and stop, you will always be in the storm. So like I instructed Joseph, keep going; press your way through because after a while, the storm will cease. Needless to say, young people were at the funeral. Still to this day, people come up to me to talk about that revelation.

I always told my son and daughter, "You are my favorite son" or "You are my favorite daughter." Alyse is a really special person. I prayed for her that God would give my wife a daughter she could walk with and spend time with in the mall. Alyse came to this world attached to her mother's hip but close to her father's heart. She would always sit on my knee and eat the food off my plate and never the food off her own. Still to this day, if there is anybody who is like me, it's Alyse. I became famous by calling her LeLe and Joseph, JoJo. I once told a revelation about Alyse.

LeLe was a strong specimen all through middle school. She came down with a sickness at the age of twelve. She lives with this sickness even today at the age of 20. Alyse was a tremendous athlete, but her sickness gave her a disability, so she couldn't practice a lot. We laugh today, because the great basketball player Alan Iverson was accused of missing practice. We would tease Alyse about practice.

Well, in high school when JoJo was a senior and LeLe was a sophomore, they played on the same night. They were both basketball players. LeLe had started since she was a freshman on the varsity team as the point guard. I had a call from the school principal that she was very ill and that I needed to pick her up. I picked her up and told her that her brother would be very concerned. She told me to tell him, "I'll meet him at home."

At the funeral I told this story to a brother who had lost his sister, and I told him the story about when pain would come to Joseph's face when his sister would get sick at school and have to leave. I would assure him always, "You can meet her at home." I told the young man at the funeral, which had lost his sister to a tragic accident, "that you can meet your sister at home."

These are the types of revelations God gives me. The Bible has stories about family, and everything God has given me I've used to glorify Him. I worked hard to train my children to honor God. The kingdom work suffered due to bad character and difficult finances, and I thought that if I had a chance to help mold and change the church, I would do so through my children. I would pour into them my love and the Bible.

My children had great accolades in academics, attitude, and athletics. Alyse graduated with honors and a 3.5 grade point average. Joseph graduated from high school with a 3.87 GPA; ninety-eight schools recruited him, and he was named the "State of Michigan 2009 Heisman Trophy Winner." A couple of my most memorable trips were to Princeton, Harvard, Northwestern, University of Chicago, and MIT. I wanted him to sign with MIT because the basketball coach really wanted him, and I knew it would probably take two more generations for a Hines to be offered the opportunity to go to MIT. On the flight back, he said some very profound words to me. He said, "Dad, you put much into me. Why do I have to go to a school where other men and women made a name to be something?"

I told him that a name brand goes a long way.

Joseph said, "I guess that's why Jesus chose the barn to be born in and not the Holiday Inn."

I left the conversation alone. We got off the plane, and I went home, knowing God had a purpose for my son. Men couldn't steal the credit for what he would become. My daughter, Alyse, struggled with her sickness. My son would ensure me that Alyse was brighter than he. Joseph scored a 27 without preparation on the ACT. LeLe had taken the ACT and hadn't received her results. We had grown, so we were able to leave her at home by herself with her sickness.

One day we came home from an event, and Alyse said to us, "I received my ACT scores," and I can remember feeling so hurt for her. I didn't want to show any disapproval. Alyse had missed 119 days of school with her sickness. She eventually graduated with a 3.5 grade point average. It wasn't in the running with her brother's 3.87. She had all the AP honor classes her brother had, but Alyse was a very sick young lady.

I shall never forget that we were standing in the bathroom as she began to tell us her ACT score. She told us she had received a 24. I thought she'd read it wrong, and I asked to see the paper. She showed it to me with some hurt in her face. I read the 24; I began to run and shout. To me Alyse had outdone her brother, even though the number didn't reveal that she had. I knew she'd achieved something many would never have been able to achieve. I was thankful to God that my daughter had achieved a high score. Many of the young people I had coached in her class had received 16 and below. Alyse had scored the highest ACT score out of all African-American children in her class. Still today she is my child of wisdom. I have appointed to her the guardianship over her brother. This is somewhat a joke because Alyse protects Joseph.

When Joseph was in the first grade, a third-grader jumped on him because Joseph had beat him in a footrace. We were walking Joseph back to the class. We had talked to the principal. LeLe asked her brother, "Joseph, where is the boy that hit you?" Joseph pointed the boy out, and before I knew it, LeLe had broken from my reach, jumped on the boy, and bit him in the face. She broke the boy's skin; blood was coming out of her mouth. I was so embarrassed, but yet I was a proud father that my children would defend each other. Still to this day LeLe approves or disapproves of Joseph's girlfriends or friends, and she oversees his finances.

Joseph is a very compassionate and kind young man. He would give you the shirt off his back if his sister would let him unbutton it.

Alyse was accepted and given an academic scholarship to MSU, and

Joseph was accepted and given an academic scholarship to Ohio State. Jim Tressel interviewed him as a prospective football player for "the" Ohio State. I wanted him to play, and he told me that he'd played sports in high school only because he'd known it made his father and mother happy and because his friends had played. It was time for him to make a choice for him, and he didn't have any friends at Ohio State, so there was no need to play anymore.

Tragedy Turned to Triumph

We dropped Alyse off at school, at MSU, on a Tuesday, August 27, 2012. We were very frightened because she had been so sick. We didn't know whether she was able to sustain and support herself away from home on her own.

But God works in mysterious ways. On August 29, 2012, a Thursday evening, we received a phone call that would forever change our lives. The Columbus Police Department had beaten our son, Joseph, across the street from the Union Building at Ohio State. It was reported that 25 officers showed up at the scene. Since one of the officers had given a 10-3 "Officer in Trouble," Joseph was charged with five counts, which added up to misdemeanors. Four of the charges were dropped, and eventually Joseph was charged and agreed to littering. He spent two days in the trauma unit at a hospital. It took us half a day to locate his whereabouts. The police wouldn't release the name of the hospital at first.

As I say, God moves in mysterious ways. Our attention turned from my daughter's sickness to our son's tragedy and rehabilitation.

Our daughter's illness is still prevalent, and she has been to doctors in Chicago, at the University of Michigan, in Cleveland, and at the Mayo Clinic in Rochester, Minnesota. But we've learned through it all that God's grace is sufficient. Our son is living with the side effects of being beaten and embarrassed. Today, as I write this, I'm on my way to take them, JoJo and LeLe, to the credit union to set them up with their first credit card for financial stability and a good name. Alyse paid her first federal taxes at the age of five, and Joseph at the age of seven. My children were given the spirit to work for everything. Render onto Caesar what is Caesar's and unto God what is God's Luke 20:25.

As I am about to close this story, my children, Joseph and Alyse, are 22 and 20, respectively. In April I called Joseph and Alyse to my bedside. I told my wife to get the children and send them into the room, one by one, as I lay in bed. I told each one of them, "I am giving you each $100,000." It is in your name now. Not to be used for college."

Joseph raised a question. "What do you want us to do with this money?"

I began to lay the plan out. "A portion of this is put aside to pay for your first house. Another portion of this is laid out for you to travel and see the country when you are in your 40s. Another portion of this is laid out for you to give away in your 50s. And another portion of this is invested so you can leave it to your heirs." I broke the $100,000 down into $25,000 for each decade. It was invested in stocks to grow over time, so when they hit those milestones in their lives, they would have a plan, as David said in Psalm 90:12. "Lord, teach us how to number our days."

End of family

The Last Word

It is with a deep sense of gratitude and wonder that I entered into this season of writing. Only our God could have sustained this pastoral journey for 30 plus years. I give Him praise and glory for the grace and mercy He has extended.

I pray that this book will be a blessing to those who read it, discuss it, and study the information. So many have given themselves to this work. I pray that in the annals of human history, it will be recorded that for 30 plus years at Lily Missionary Baptist Church there stood a man and woman of God who had a heart for God and a desire to see God's will come to pass in the lives of the people.

May God bless each and every one of you who have put your hands to this ministry endeavor. I pray that your labor will be rewarded and that your sacrifice will yield magnificent manifestations, which will bring you unspeakable joy.

The last words of my dying father on his bed were, "James, finish what you started." So to those who stood with me, may our blessed Savior stand with you. To my dedicated wife, my beloved son, and my daughter, I shall be eternally grateful. May His face shine upon you because of Calvary." Love James

Pastor T. ....
Chairman, Trustee Ministry

1117 WADE STREET
JACKSON, MICHIGAN, 49201

Church Phone 783-5568
Residence Phone 787-4924

REVEREND JAMES L. HINES, PASTOR

March 19, 1999

Dear Lily Missionary Baptist Church:

I Pastor James L Hines and Sister Leontyne C. Hines has agreed in spirit to pay the Lily church family the sum of 100,000 dollars, 50,000 to be pay on 3/21/1999 and the second portion of 50,000 at retirement or death of Pastor Hines. The Payment will be made through a insurance policy supplied by State Farm Life Insurance Company, Policy number LF-1607-0235.

Because of Calvary...

Rev. James L Hines

[signature]

Leontyne C. Hines

[signature]

Witness

[signature: Glorie Peterson]

**The words of his wife,
We've come here poor, we can leave poor.**

Brandon Gibbs, Kauma Doye, Pastor Hines, Tim Williams, Coy Boyer, Michael Scot – cleaning the land for the new church – 2000

These young men joined Pastor Hines after 26 days.

Pastor Hines,

Please accept this as a faith gift. My wife, Shawnna, and I are excited about what God is doing at Lily Missionary Baptist Church, and how He is using you and your family in His work. I pray that you will **NOT BE DISCOURAGED**, but you will be *Encouraged* as you see God supply the need. Thank you for allowing my family to be a part of what God is doing.

In His Name
Tim Hampton

President Bill Clinton, Pastor Hines, and Senator Schauer – 2014 Battle Creek, MI, Private Setting

My Question, How should a young man save his money? The President's response..."Pay as you go."

JACKSON HIGH SCHOOL

544 WILDWOOD AVENUE · JACKSON, MICHIGAN 49201 · PHONE: 517-784-4501

April 1, 1999

Reverend James Hines, Pastor
Lily Baptist Church
1117 Deyo
Jackson, MI 49201

Dear Pastor Hines:

Please find enclosed a donation to your future building project at the Lily Baptist
Church, in particular, the youth center that will provide services for young people
here in Jackson. Your vision and dedication to the realization of that vision is
remarkable. I want you to know that Jackson High School is in complete support
of you and what you do for young people here. Keep up the good work!

Sincerely,

Thomas J. Stobie
Principal
Jackson High School

A CMS Energy Company

212 West Michigan Avenue
Jackson, MI 49201-2277

tel: 517 788 0432
Fax: 517 788 2281

Carolyn A. Bloodworth
Secretary/Treasurer
CONSUMERS
ENERGY
FOUNDATION

December 18, 1999

Reverend James L Hines
Lily Missions Center
1117 G. W. Wade Drive
Jackson, MI 49201

Dear Reverend Hines:

I am pleased to inform you the Board of Directors of the Consumers Energy Foundation recently approved a $20,000 grant to support construction of the Lily Missions Center. This grant is payable over a period of four years, beginning with a $5,000 installment payable in 2000. This grant and its first payment are contingent upon submission of a three- to five-year business plan for the center. Upon receipt of this plan and evidence of sustainability for the future, we will issue the first grant check. Please submit this plan to me at the address listed above.

Any recognition you provide for this grant should be credited to the *Consumers Energy Foundation*. I would also appreciate receiving a copy of any correspondence or news releases you may issue to publicize this grant. Before we will issue the remaining three installments of $5,000 each, I ask that you provide us with an update on the status of the project and an accounting of the use of our funding. I would like this information no later than December 15 of 2000, 2001 and 2002.

Thank you again, for your interest in Consumers Energy and for providing us with an opportunity to support this important project. Please accept my best wishes for continued success in your efforts to provide outreach programs and services for our community.

Sincerely,

Carolyn

CC: RGStuart
      KAMcCarthy

Have a wonderful holiday!

The Jackson Community Foundation

230 West Michigan Avenue Jackson, Michigan 49201 (517) 787-1321 Fax (517) 787-4333

January 14, 2000

Rev. James L. Hines
Lily Missionary Baptist Church
1117 G. W. Wade Dr.
Jackson, MI 49201

Dear Rev. Hines,

Enclosed, please find check #008611 in the amount of $50,000. This represents payment of a recent grant to the Lily Missions Center for the construction of the youth center.

Congratulations.

Sincerely,

Carolyn M. Pratt
Dir. of Programs and Youth Services

HURST FOUNDATION   1600 HATCH RD
JACKSON, MI   49201   517   783 2119   FAX   789 8165

Jun 2, 2000

Lilly Missions Center
1117 G W Wade Dr
Jackson, Michigan 49203

**He served with his
Heart and Mind.**

Gentlemen:

The Hurst Foundation is committing $300,000 to the Lilly
Center over the next 3 years on a matching basics; 2:1 every
2 received the foundation will pay 1 up to 100,000 per year
matching revenue received during that year toward the
construction of the new complex.

Sincerely,

A P Hurst
President

73

November 22, 2000

Reverend James L. Hines
President, Lily Missions Center
1117 G.W. Wade Drive
Jackson, MI 49201

Dear Reverend Hines:

I am very pleased to be able to make a $20,000.00 donation this year from The   Fund. As I had mentioned to you earlier, this donation was to be split between the   Memorial Fund and The   Fund. However, The Jackson Community Foundation has new restrictions on the amount that can be taken from earnings, so I will fulfill my pledge from   alone.

Your speech at the JCF dinner last weekend was so inspirational. You are truly the most moving speaker I have ever heard.

Best Regards,

Weatherwax Foundation
Weatherwax

Dedicated to the support of Education, Civic & Social Programs, Culture, Science, & the Arts.

November 1, 2000

The man I call Dad, the mentor.

Dear Pastor Hines:

We are pleased to inform you that the Trustees have decided to commit $400,000 to the Lily Missions Center project. The terms of this grant are as follows:

   A. $155,000 will be paid forthwith. $45,000 will be paid
       to the Center to cover costs in connection with a
       Director of Grants and Finance, as soon as he/she is
       on the job.

   B. $100,000 will be paid on October 1, 2001, conditioned
       upon your obtaining additional contributions in the
       amount of $100,000 over and above the $227,000+ you
       are now showing.

   C. $100,000 will be paid on October 1, 2002, conditioned
       upon your obtaining additional contributions in the
       amount of $100,000 over and above the $225,000+ you
       are now showing.

In addition, we have consulted the Directors of Weatherwax Investment Company and, upon your request in writing, they will commit to a $100,000 grant payable January 2, 2001.

One condition for receiving the payments beyond the $155,000 emergency payment shall be a satisfactory arrangement with the mortgage holder for a separation of the mortgage debt between your church project and the Missions Center project.

Yours very truly,

WEATHERWAX FOUNDATION

Lawrence L. Bullen
Trustee

...protecting your tomorrows

September 20, 2000

Reverend James L. Hines
Lily Missionary Baptist Church
P.O. Box 421
Jackson, MI 49201

Dear Reverend Hines:

We have a framed photo in our office with the saying "A hundred years from now it will not matter what my bank account was, the sort of house I lived in, or the kind of car I drove.... But the world may be different because I was important in the life of a child."

Truly this is God's hope for mankind.

I will pledge $3,000.00 payable over the next three years to your dream for our children.

I salute your efforts and your enthusiasm.

Sincerely,

Eric B. Walton, CIC
President

McGOWAN ELECTRIC SUPPLY, INC.

425 LIBERTY ST.
P.O. BOX 765
JACKSON, MI 49204-0765
PHONE (517) 782-9301

1153 W. BEECHER ST.
ADRIAN, MI 49221
PHONE (517) 263-5500

May 26, 2000

Reverend James Hines
Lily Missionary Baptist Church
1117 Wade Dr.
Jackson,MI 49203

Dear Reverend Hines,

Enclosed is McGowan Electric Supply's check for
$2,500. toward the development of the Lily Missionary
Community Center.

We pledge to repeat this contribution in each of the
following three years, for a total donation of $10,000.

We are pleased to contribute to this exciting
project,

Sincerely,

Mike McGowan
President

Jackson High School
Track and Field

March 23, 2000

Dear Reverend Hines,

I want to thank you for the support of Jackson High School, most specifically, the track and field program. I know that you encouraged a number of young people to get involved in the program and your work has paid off. We presently have 57 boys and 33 girls on the track team. Hopefully, most will stay.

Also, thank you for the use of the vans during the indoor track season. The vans made it possible to take a number of young people to the meets who may not have been able to go had it not been for your generosity. I am enclosing a check as a donation toward your center project as small token of our appreciation for the use of the vans.

THANKS again for all that you do.

Sincerely,

Jerry Reis
Head Track Coach

August 30, 2000

Rev. James L. Hines
Lily Missionary Baptist Church
1117 G.W. Wade Drive
Jackson, Michigan 49201

RE: **Lily Mission Center**

Dear James:

On behalf of the   Fund, please find enclosed a check in the amount of $25,000.00 payable to the Lily Mission Center.

In accordance with our previous discussions and your grant request, this will confirm that these funds are to be used exclusively for the Lily Mission Center with respect to construction and/or youth programs conducted by the Lily Mission Center.

The terms of the grant require that within one year, you write to the trustees and confirm that the funds were used for the purposes set forth above. It is very likely that additional funds may be available in the future, and our future contributions will be determined by your response.

Since we do not wish to solicit requests for grants or donations, we ask that for public purposes, this grant be considered anonymous.

Yours truly,

VALERIE L. BULLEN
3829 GUEST ROAD
JACKSON, MICHIGAN 49203

November 29, 2000

Mr. Ed Idziak
Salomon Smith Barney, Inc.
3101 Spring Arbor Road
Jackson, MI 49203

Dear Mr. Idziak:

Re: Donation of AT&T Corp. Stock to Lily Missions Center

In line with your telephone conversation with my husband, Lawrence L. Bullen, of November 28, enclosed please find Certificate No. TX271748 of AT&T Corp. evidencing 60 common shares of the corporation. It is my understanding that Lily Missions Center has an account with your firm which is the appropriate recipient for donations of securities. Accordingly, please transfer the 60 shares covered by the referenced certificate to the account of Lily Mission Center, constituting a gift from me to the center.

Please be in touch with Pastor James Hines relative to your handling of this donation.

Yours very truly,

Valerie L. Bullen

Valerie L. Bullen

cc: Rev. James Hines

Jackson County
community foundation
For **good**. For **ever.**

January 24, 2001

The Reverend James L. Hines
Lily Missionary Baptist Church
1117 G.W. Wade Drive
Jackson, MI 49201

Dear Reverend Hines,

Enclosed please find check #009408 in the amount of $25,000 from The Jackson County Community Foundation. This represents the second and final payment of a $75,000 grant to the Lily Mission Center for the development of its youth center. Thank you for the update on the progress of program development for the Center.

Sincerely,

Kimball Cartwright
Program Officer

Wetherby Funeral Home
Funeral Directors Since 1895

October 16, 2000

Dear Pastor Hines,

Cris and I enjoyed meeting with you the other day over lunch and hearing about the construction of the Youth Center. We agree with you, this will not only have a positive affect on our community now, but it will also impact our community for generations to come.

We are proud to be able to join hands with you to help in carrying some of the financial responsibility for such a project as this. Therefore, Wetherby Funeral Home will be giving a gift of $10,000.00 to Lily Missionary Baptist Church, for the Youth Center. This gift will be given over the next five (5) years, at a rate of $2,000.00 per year, beginning January of 2001.

Please accept this gift as a token of our appreciation to you and your church family, as we all endeavor to provide quality service to our community.

Sincerely,

D. Cris Pelham   Tim Hampton

Weatherwax Foundation

Weatherwax

Dedicated to the support of Education, Civic & Social Programs, Culture, Science, & the Arts

November 2, 2000

Rev. James L. Hines
Lily Missions Center
1117 W.G. Wade Drive
Jackson, MI 49201

Dear Rev. Hines,

The Trustees of the Weatherwax Foundation, attorney Lawrence Bullen and Thomas Mitchell of Comerica Bank, are pleased to confirm completion of a wire transfer in the amount of $155,000, on Thursday November 2, 2000, to Midwest Construction toward payment of a portion of the costs related to construction of the Lily Missions Center. We look forward to working with you in the coming months.

Sincerely,

(Mrs.) Maria Miceli Dotterweich
Executive Director

c. Trustees

November 30, 2016

Dear Reverend Hines:

Enclosed please find a check for $ 19,000.00 to support the many missions at Lily.

By cashing this check, Lily Missions Center agrees to: credit Speckhard Knight Charitable Foundation (SKCF) in any press releases and and annual reports; notify SKCF of any material changes to your IRS 501 c 3 designation; and submit a report , via US mail, of the funds usages and the successes the monies generated.

Merry Christmas!

In Christ,

Gerald Knight

Gerald Knight

Pastor Hines selling
lots for $500,000

Jackson
community foundation
For Jackson. For **good**. For ever.

June 15, 2017

Pastor James L. Hines
C/O Lily Missions Center
1117 W.G. Wade Drive
Jackson, MI 49202

Pastor Hines,

On behalf of Jackson Community Foundation Board of Trustees and Staff, I commend your efforts over the many years to make a community's dream into reality. It is with great pleasure that we celebrate your success in building a quality youth center that has had a meaningful impact on our community. You have continued your commitment to support youth in their efforts to grow educationally, spiritually and in character by investing in a coordinator of youth services.

As a testament to the trust you have built, the Jackson Community Foundation and its many donors have been please to support this work, both the capital campaign for the center and the startup and ongoing services you provide to the youth in our community.

With a thankful heart,

Monica Moser

49201, tel (517) 787-1321 fax (517) 787-4333 email jcf@jacksoncf.org, we

86

Bring high profile individuals to town to help children.

Pastor Hines, Coach Dungy, and Coach Fairly.

National President's first time in Michigan preaching as President. October 2016, Lily Missionary Baptist Church

July 18, 2017

Reverend James Hines
Lily Missionary Baptist Church
P.O. Box 421
Jackson, Michigan 49204

Dear Reverend Hines,

I praise and thank God for you and the work that the Lily Mission Center does in Jackson, Michigan and the surrounding area. As President of the National Baptist Convention, USA, Inc., be assured of my prayers for you, the church and the effort of the Mission Center as you live out the biblical mission of servanthood.

It is our prayer that the grace of God will continue to allow you to be a beacon of light and hope to the many persons you have served and will serve. As the Apostle Paul said to the church, be steadfast, unmovable always abounding in the work of the Lord, knowing that your labor is not in vain.

Yours in the mission and ministry of Christ,

Jerry Young

bj

June 16, 2017

Rev. James L. Hines, President
Lily Missions Center
P.O. Box 421
Jackson, MI 49204

Dear Rev. Hines,

The Trustees of the Weatherwax Foundation, Chairman Larry Bullen and Comerica Bank, reviewed your request for support of the pay-down of the Lily Missions Center mortgage debt. They have approved a $75,000 challenge grant to be provided when LMC has raised the necessary additional $250,000 in gifts to complete the mortgage pay-down. We include in that figure the amount of $112,000 already committed as outlined in your grant submission, which leaves LMC $138,000 to raise. This challenge grant is only available until September 1, 2017 because, as you know, we are closing. Good luck with this important effort.

Regards,

(Mrs.) Maria Miceli Dotterweich
Executive Director

C. Weatherwax Trustees

A challenge "to finish what you started."

Running into the fire

Leap of Faith
By Linda Hass

Dentistry at Lily

Before Pastor James Hines was born, his mother ran into a burning house to save her children. She was able to retrieve one, getting badly burned in the process, but lost two in the blaze because firemen held her back from going into the house a second time.

The rescue made a strong impression on Hines, the senior pastor of Lily Mission Baptist Church, who uses it as a model for taking God-ordained leaps of faith today.

"To my mother, running into a burning building wasn't a risk--it was a necessity. I feel the same way about today's youth. In many ways, they are on fire, burning from the destruction caused by drugs, by fatherless homes, and by lack of guidance. I believe God has called me to run into the fire and save them," he said.

For Hines, running into the fire has meant, among other things, going out on a limb financially. "I had a vision from God 17 years ago of a center where youth could get off the street, learn life skills, improve their grades, play sports and benefit from mentorships and scholarships," he said.

So the intrepid pastor woke his wife, Leontyne, in the middle of the night and posed an unlikely question: would she consider giving up their life savings of $56,000 to start a youth center? He still remembers her affirmative reply: "We've come here poor and we can leave here poor."

The couple's seed money, combined with a loan and other contributions, financed construction of the 20,000 square foot Lily Mission Center, which opened April 2001. Today the center, which is next to the church, hosts after-school and summer reading programs, sports events and extracurricular activities for participants ranging from pre-school to 21 years old.

Kristie Morris is one of many who benefitted from Hines' calling. When her mother died unexpectedly, Hines provided guidance and helped her find scholarship money to attend Central Michigan University. Morris not only graduated from CMU, she received Teacher of the Year accolades when she worked at Dibble Elementary School several years ago, Hines said.

Safe Place at Lily

"Pastor Hines wants people to succeed and is dedicated to youth," said Morris, who has since moved to California with her husband. "He won't do the work for you, but he will give you the information and guide you to get it done."

The center's students include a former homeless youth who also works as a teacher, a pastor, an accountant and a lawyer. By all accounts, the center is a success, but Hines is not about to rest on his laurels. The confidant pastor is now taking his next leap--spearheading an initiative to pay off the center's mortgage. "Closing the debt will free up $78,000 per year, which will allow us to offer more programs for youth," said Hines.

To that end, Hines sought--and received--a $75,000 challenge grant from the Weatherwax Foundation. The grant is contingent on the center's ability to pay off the balance of its mortgage--$250,000--before the Foundation closes on Sept. 1.

"I believe that the God who paved the way for the Center to exist in the first place will continue to bless it," said Hines, who is coordinating an Aug. 31 debt retirement fund raiser celebration called "Lily Taste of Gratitude." The all-day event will include free food, entertainment, and a worship service from 7-9 p.m.

Working the Garden at Lily

Hosting a fund raiser the day before grant money expires might seem risky for some, but not for this bold pastor, who is poised to publish a book titled "I Believe Him" sometime this summer. "I want to show people that the more you trust God, the more your faith grows, and the more your faith grows, the more he can work through you."

Jackson resident Wally Niecko said he has been so impressed with the center's positive impact on youth, and with Hines' bold spirit, that he gave a significant donation to the center--and Niecko doesn't even attend Lily Mission Baptist Church.

"Pastor Hines is going out of his way to help Jackson's youth," Niecko said. "I want to support that.

Factoid

Those interested in making a contribution to the Lily Missions Center can donate online by clicking the donation link at: https://www.lilymissionscenter.org , or send a check, payable to "Lily Mission Center," to Lily Mission Center, P.O. Box 421, Jackson, Mich., 49204.

U of M Wellness Program at Lily   Orchestra at Lily   Feeding the Community

Credit: Linda Hass, *The Exponent*

Printed in the United States
By Bookmasters